T0209379

GRATEFUL

In Love with My Messy Beautiful Life

Poems and Other Writings

ALINA ADAMUT

BALBOA.PRESS
A DIVISION OF HAY HOUSE

Cover/Graphic Design: Ioana Cretu

Balboa Press books may be ordered through booksellers or by contacting:

Balboa Press
A Division of Hay House
1663 Liberty Drive
Bloomington, IN 47403
www.balboapress.com
844-682-1282

Because of the dynamic nature of the Internet, any web addresses or links contained in this book may have changed since publication and may no longer be valid. The views expressed in this work are solely those of the author and do not necessarily reflect the views of the publisher, and the publisher hereby disclaims any responsibility for them.

The author of this book does not dispense medical advice or prescribe the use of any technique as a form of treatment for physical, emotional, or medical problems without the advice of a physician, either directly or indirectly. The intent of the author is only to offer information of a general nature to help you in your quest for emotional and spiritual well-being. In the event you use any of the information in this book for yourself, which is your constitutional right, the author and the publisher assume no responsibility for your actions.

Print information available on the last page.

ISBN: 978-1-9822-4789-8 (sc)
ISBN: 978-1-9822-5489-6 (e)

Library of Congress Control Number: 2020917639

Balboa Press rev. date: 09/29/2020

To my boys:

Marius,

my favorite person,

and David,

my favorite tattoo on my heart

A day

we do not

say, think,

or feel a

Thank you

for

someone or

something,

is

a day

wasted.

Contents

Introduction.. xv

Grateful for Everything xvii

Chapter 1: Nature 1

Grateful for Nature 2

Grateful for Air... 3

Grateful for Trees 4

Grateful for Fire... 6

Grateful for Wind 7

Grateful for Sunsets 8

Grateful for Water 9

Thank You, Nature 10

Dear Reader 11

Chapter 2: Colors 13

Grateful for All Things White 14

Grateful for All Things Blue...15

Grateful for All Things Green 16

Grateful for All Things Red 17

Grateful for All Things Yellow......................................18

Grateful for All Things Brown 19

Grateful for All Colors 21

Dear Reader 22

Chapter 3: My People..23

Thankful for My Mother..24

Thankful for My Father...26

Thankful for My Parents...27

Thankful for My Marius 28

Thankful for My Favorite Tattoo on My Heart 29

Thankful for Deep Conversations with My David...... 30

Grateful for My Brother's Family 31

Grateful for Children.. 32

Grateful for My Friends 33

Thankful for My Romanian Community 34

Grateful for My Overseas Friends............................. 36

Thankful for My Little Family.....................................37

Dear Reader 38

Chapter 4: Inspirational People 39

Grateful for Artists... 40

Grateful for Ioana Cretu 41

Grateful for Oprah..42

Grateful for Teachers 44

Grateful for Laurie Ventura 45

Grateful for Special Education Teachers 46

Grateful for Tina Sosna..47

Ode to Tree Shadows 49

Grateful for Don 50

My Book's Angel 52

Grateful for All the People Who Inspire Me 54

Dear Reader 57

Chapter 5: Pieces of Me.....................................59

Grateful for My Body... 60

Grateful for My Soul.. 62

Grateful for My Imperfections 64

Grateful for My Gifts.. 65

Grateful for Being an Extrovert and an Introvert....... 66

Grateful for My Most Memorable Encounters........... 67

Grateful for My Silliness 68
Dear Reader 69

Chapter 6: Messy Beautiful Life............................ 71

Her Story.. 72
A Reminder 74
Grateful for Wake-Up Calls..75
Let's Always Give Thanks... 77
Yes..78
Thankful for Being Bigger than My Challenges 79
Dear Reader 80

Chapter 7: Life Lessons 81

Grateful for Being Enough 82
Grateful for Finding My Home...................................... 83
Grateful for Being Okay with Not Being Okay........... 84
Thankful for Welcoming Change 85
Grateful for Recognizing My Power 86
Thankful for Being Whole 87
Grateful for Learning to Fill My Own Bucket............. 88
Thankful for Possibilities.. 89
Dear Reader 90

Chapter 8: Unlikely Thank-Yous........................... 91

Grateful for Soul Pain... 92
Grateful for Beautiful Strangers 94
Grateful for the In-Between Moments....................... 96
Grateful for Mind Striptease..97
Grateful for Mondays 100
Unlikely Thank-Yous...102
Dear Reader 103

Chapter 9: Simple Pleasures of Life................. 105

Grateful for Books 106

Grateful for Music...108

Grateful for Dance...110

"Dance for All of Us, Alina" 111

Grateful for Handwritten Letters 112

Grateful for Photographers 113

Grateful for TV Comedy Shows............................... 114

Looking Deeply 115

Grateful for the Joy of Being 117

Dear Reader 118

Chapter 10: Extraordinary Days 119

Grateful for Glimpses of Heaven.............................120

Holding David for the First Time 121

Grateful for Trips 122

Grateful for Poems Born on Trips 124

The Fifteenth Wedding Anniversary 125

Grateful for My Joy Festival 127

Mother's Day at Longwood Gardens 128

Dear Reader 130

Chapter 11: Places 131

Grateful for My Garden 132

Thank You, New York City 133

Grateful for Tula Yoga 134

Grateful for Deep Cut Gardens................................136

Grateful for Holmdel Park 137

Grateful for My Favorite Place: My Heart.................139

Dear Reader 140

Chapter 12: Remain Grateful............................... 141

Grateful for All New Things.....................................142

Being Grateful Is a Choice......................................144

Grateful for Today 145

Embrace the Mystery...146

Thank You for Your Beauty 147

Thank You, Dear Reader...151

Introduction

Good habits enhance the quality of our lives. I am familiar with some of them: praying, meditating, practicing yoga and mindfulness, spending time outdoors, eating healthfully, helping others, exercising, being exposed to inspirational people and materials, and journaling. I practice these from time to time; some of them more than the others. I agree with Gretchen Rubin: "What you do every day matters more than what you do once in a while."

Consciously showing gratitude is my best practice and my number-one good habit! I give thanks daily. I give thanks many times during the day.

I give thanks at two specific moments each day: when I wake up ("Thank you for being alive," "Thank you for this day," "Thank you for my breath") and at night, when I give thanks together with my family.

Many times during the day, spontaneous thank-yous arise in my heart and in my mind. Conscious daily thank-yous are propelled by my desire to acknowledge the multitude of reasons I have to feel blessed.

The best rewards of living as much as possible in a mental state of gratitude are those magical moments when I am completely content with my life—with all of it!

Being grateful saves me during hard times and improves my life each day. Giving thanks keeps my life beautiful, light, and full of goodness.

Please join me on a journey through my garden of gratitude. Thank you!

Grateful for Everything

It's so easy;
it's so natural
to give thanks
for good health,
for family, friends, nice houses,
for food, trips, music, surprises, gifts,
for sun, nature, good news, smiles, our kids' hugs,
for romantic moments, and good times.

Nowadays, I am learning to give thanks
for soul pain,
for unfulfilled wishes,
for disappointments,
for anger,
for anxiety, and
for all the things we call "bad" or "negative."

All the trials are blessings in disguise.
They have a remarkable capacity to catapult us
closer to our true selves,
closer to our essence.

Challenges are our best teachers.
They are meant to teach us
some great life lessons about
compassion,
tolerance,
patience,
understanding,
humility,
gentleness,
forgiveness,
generosity,
respect,
bravery, and
gratitude.

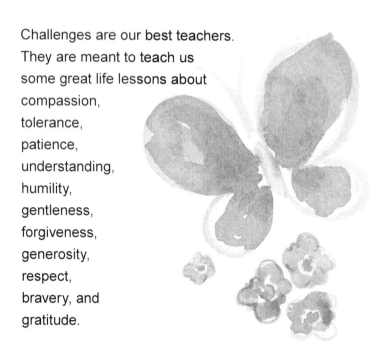

Obstacles are opportunities to better ourselves.
We are here on earth
to learn our lessons
and, more importantly, to live our lessons.

CHAPTER 1

NATURE

Grateful for Nature

Being in a forest,
being on the beach,
being by a waterfall,
being on a path up the mountain,
being near a lake,
being under a big old tree,
being in a wildflower field,
being in nature feels like home to me.

Being
outdoors—
what a treat
to my soul.
What a delight.

Grateful for Air

Grateful for the crisp mountain air,
for the salty, breezy ocean air.

Grateful for the air we all share,
the air inside me, and the air around me.

Grateful for the early spring air that makes us
fall in love with life again and again each year.

Grateful for the cool air indoors on a torrid summer day,
for the rushed air we all call wind.

Grateful for the air that continues to exist even when
I feel breathless because something beautiful—a
moment, a person, or an experience—steals my heart
for a little while.

"Thank you for my breath,"
my favorite morning mantra.

Air, dear,
I cannot see you,
I cannot taste you,
I cannot smell you,
but I feel you, and
I am grateful for you!

Grateful for Trees

Every tree is a giving tree.
Trees share stories
about being strong and flexible,
about history and living in the now.

Every tree is a giving tree.
Trees give the best hugs
when nobody is watching
and the best advice too.

Every tree is a giving tree.
Trees reach up to the sky;
their arms, tall branches,
praying for us.

Every tree is a giving tree.
Trees invite us to rest in their shade,
offer us flowers, and
spoil us with juicy fruits.

Every tree is a giving tree.
In fall, trees teach us
about the beauty of
letting go.

Every tree is a giving tree.
Trees keep speaking to my soul,
calling me often
into the woods.

Trees sow beautiful seeds
into my heart.
In another lifetime,
I would love to come back as a tree.

Grateful for Fire

Fire, you seduce me
with your warmth,
with your colors,
with the way you whirl your body.

Fire, I am fascinated by you.
I could watch your dance for a long time.
When I look at you,
time loses its grip on me.

Fire, thank you for cooking our meals,
for warming our houses,
for adding charm to our camping trips,
to our lives.

Dear Fire,
Thank you for creating cozy areas
where a sleeping cat and a bookworm
can meet and snuggle.

Grateful for Wind

Blowing softly,
three ivory shirts sway
on the line outside.
The sun is hiding in my eyes.

Yesterday a little, dreamy girl
had magic wind
playing in her hair.
Eyes closed, a princess came to life.

Today you shove the woman I become
down the slopes at Sandy Hook.
Arms become wings.
Whee! I'm flying on my Rollerblades.

Dear Crazy Wind,
Thank you for being powerful and gentle,
invisible and cool.
Some hours a terrific poet,
some hours a fearless warrior.

Grateful for Sunsets

Sunset dissolves in my blood.
My whole being accepts the celestial offering.

Hummingbirds navigate my arteries.
Polar bears crawl in my capillaries.

Flowers arise from my earth.
Three pioneers plant a flag in my heart.

Sunset becomes restless inside me.
My blood splashes the horizon.
I am infinite beauty!

Grateful for Water

Lakes, rivers, oceans,
seas, streams, creeks, and
waterfalls.
My seven wonders.

Thankful for our blue earth's precious treasure.
Thankful for our daily refreshing drink.
Thankful for the sound of flowing water.
Thankful for the rain, snow, dew, and tears.

Dear Water,
Thank you for cleaning our bodies,
our dishes, our clothes.
Thank you for making possible swimming,
diving, sailing, fishing.
Thank you for allowing seeds to become flowers,
trees, fruits, vegetables, grass.
Thank you for growing life!

Thank You, Nature

I am married to the sky.
I am a bride of the sea.
I am engaged to the forest.
I am the mistress of the sunrise.
I am madly in love with the morning mist.
I just eloped; Mr. River and I are crazy about each other.
I am falling deeply for a yellow butterfly.
I have a huge crush on an old oak.

Oh my!
My love life is so busy.

Dear Reader

Next time you find yourself in nature,
please notice the bark of a sturdy tree trunk.
Touch it, feel its grounding power,
and whisper, "Thank you."

Take a deep breath by a lake or
by a riverbank.
Allow the river to carry all your worries away.
Offer it a heartfelt, "Thank you."

Walk a bit slower on a forest path.
Take in all the beauty around you.
Close your eyes for five seconds.
Let the gratitude wash all over you.

What's your favorite place in nature?
Picture yourself in that special heaven.
Remember what you feel when you are there; smile.
Say, "Thank you."

CHAPTER 2

COLORS

Grateful for All Things White

Grateful for the gentle flowers called snowdrops.

Grateful for little ballerinas in white tutus.

Grateful for my sweet white cat, Daisy.

Grateful for white sheets drying in the wind.

Grateful for snowflakes dancing in the sky.

Grateful for white pages heavy with possibilities.

Grateful for white, wrinkled hands resting on a table.

Grateful for a white-haired uncle smiling for no reason.

Grateful for blizzards swirling the snowfields.

Grateful for milk, our first food.

Grateful for white, puffy clouds.

Grateful for white, dreamy dresses.

Grateful for white tablecloths.

Grateful for lit white candles.

Grateful for vases with white peonies.

Grateful for blowing dandelions, playful white fluff.

Grateful for a joyous bride running in a cotton field.

Grateful for white's song expressing quietness, light, innocence, peacefulness, purity, and infinity.

Grateful for All Things Blue

Grateful for our blue planet.
Grateful for the vast Atlantic Ocean nearby.
Grateful for blue being a summer feast for my eyes.
Grateful for all turquoise seas and lakes.
Grateful for the marvelous azure sky, my dear playdate.
Grateful for forget-me-nots hiding in the tall grass.
Grateful for all cerulean flowers.
Grateful for my goddaughter Juliana's eyes.
Grateful for yummy blueberries.
Grateful for concord grapes from our garden.
Grateful for elderberries and plums.
Grateful for cute robin eggs.
Grateful for the blue moon, a rare, beautiful surprise.
Grateful for feeling blue sometimes.
Grateful for blue jeans, cool and comfy.
Grateful for blue butterflies.
Grateful for bluebirds flying high on my sky.

Dear Blue,
Thank you for adding
serenity to my life.
Thank you for being
a therapeutic color,
a calming presence,
a joy.
Thank you for your gifts!

Grateful for All Things Green

Grateful for green hills.
Grateful for valleys covered in baby green grass.
Grateful for forests.
Grateful for green leaves talking to each other.
Grateful for moss hugging the tree trunks.
Grateful for luxurious rain forests.
Grateful for my Italian goddaughters' eyes.
Grateful for ferns, basil, parsley, dill, cilantro.
Grateful for green apples, green grapes, kiwi.
Grateful for salad, avocados, cucumbers.
Grateful for all green vegetables and fruits.
Grateful for four-leaf clovers.

Grateful for giving myself the green light to live life to the fullest.

Dear Green,
You are a relaxing color,
a symbol of life and growth.
You are full of energy.
You are a fresh and harmonious color.
Thank you for inviting peace
into my soul every single time
I encounter you in nature.

Grateful for All Things Red

Grateful for poppy fields.
Grateful for ladybugs.
Grateful for strawberries and tomatoes.
Grateful for blushing faces and for lips.
Grateful for my mama's red dress, a silky dream.
Grateful for women's monthly discharge of blood.
Grateful for red rooftops.
Grateful for red as a symbol of love.
Grateful for stop signs and for red lights.
Grateful for red wine and for red roses.
Grateful for Christ's blood, shed for all of us.
Grateful for red as the color of Christmas.
Grateful for cardinals, for rubies, and for Elmo.
Grateful for watermelon slices and for hearts.

Dear Red,
You reveal life in its splendor and in its brutality.
You are a screaming color,
a color of extremes,
a strong, passionate color,
a pretty, confident color that drives us crazy sometimes.
Red, dear,
Thank you for
churning the beauty and the beast
in one irresistible color.

Grateful for All Things Yellow

Grateful for our glorious sun.

Grateful for our brilliant moon.

Grateful for sunflowers, daffodils, dandelions.

Grateful for yellow crocuses, yellow tulips, yellow roses.

Grateful for school buses, lemons.

Grateful for baby chicks, corn on the cob.

Grateful for scrambled eggs, cheese, bananas.

Grateful for yellow dresses on my sun-kissed skin.

Grateful for New York City cabs.

Grateful for the yellow submarine.

Grateful for my yellow living room.

Grateful for days bathed in sunshine.

Grateful for yellow dry leaves singing under my steps.

Grateful for feeling sunny inside.

Dear Yellow,

You are such a bright, warm, shiny, and positive color.

Thank you for coloring my life.

Thank you for giving my journey,

your optimistic and happy vibe.

Thank you for always smiling!

Grateful for All Things Brown

Grateful for my brown eyes.
Grateful for your brown hair.
Grateful for her brown skin.
Grateful for chocolate.
Grateful for brown horses, brown bears, snails, and bees.
Grateful for all brown beings.
Grateful for the brown soil.
Grateful for coffee.
Grateful for brownies.
Grateful for chocolate cake.
Grateful for chocolate chip cookies.
Grateful for tree trunks.
Grateful for bread, pretzels, and brown beans.
Grateful for brown paper bags.
Grateful for tree cones.
Grateful for wooden constructions.
Grateful for roasted chestnuts.
Grateful for chocolate (yes, once again).

Grateful for brown,
an earthy and
a warm color.

Brown symbolizes
steadfastness,
simplicity,
friendliness.

It may not be as pretty as
its bright, happy siblings,
but it's the color of so many
delicious things and
beautiful beings.

Grateful for All Colors

Grateful for my colorful life canvas.
Grateful for our colorful human family.
Grateful for my colorful dreams.
Grateful for our colorful memories.
Grateful for my colorful journey.
Grateful for our colorful blessings.
Grateful for my colorful heart.
Grateful for our colorful encounters.

Grateful for
happy rainbows,
violet bouquets,
orange skies,
black tuxedos,
pink dresses,
gray luggage,
beige houses,
multicolor gardens.

Grateful for living in a colorful, beautiful world.

Dear Reader

What color speaks to your heart?
Do you often dress in that color?
Do you notice it a lot around you?
What do you feel when you are
surrounded by that specific color?

Give thanks for your color.
Say its name.
Write it across the sky.
Be grateful for it.

CHAPTER 3

MY PEOPLE

Thankful for My Mother

Mama, what a wonderful, unique name you have. You are my first inspiration to live fully. I inherited your gift to make friends easily wherever I go and, at the same time, to develop strong, long-lasting relationships. I inherited your gift of being able to ease someone else's burden just by being there for them, just by giving them the opportunity to share their story.

Mama, you have always inspired me to travel to new destinations and to explore the outdoors. From you, dear Mama, I inherited the great gift of counting my blessings at the end of every single trip, the gift of feeling rich because of my travel experiences. You inspire me to go beyond my comfort zone, to be curious about other cultures, different traditions, to see beauty in diversity.

Mama, you showed me how to savor music, theater, all kinds of art. Through your love of books, you kept cultivating in me the desire to be a bookworm myself, to journey to faraway places and times without actually leaving my reading nook.

One of my dearest memories is the moment I introduced you to my sweet boy, to your grandson. I vividly remember the precious hour when I gently placed baby David in your arms, a special present from me, a brand-new mama, to you, my mama.

Beautiful mother, as the famous Romanian song says, "You are my first Heaven" (Mirabela Dauer). Thank you for teaching me to live fully. Thank you for inspiring me. Dear mama, may God give you many more chances to share your light!

Thankful for My Father

Dear Dad, thank you for making me possible! Tata, you've always been in love with words. Nowadays you spend many hours solving crossword puzzles.

Dad, I inherited your passion for words. Also, I inherited your sensibility and your skills for writing poetry. I remember my surprise and the joy when I stumbled upon a romantic poem you wrote to Mama in your twenties.

Dear Dad, these two gifts—being softhearted and the gift of putting tender things down on paper—are so very precious to me. Thank you so very much! I truly appreciate the ability to feel deeply and the ability to write with my soul.

Yes, you are a gentle father, and I am aware many people do not see this as a desirable quality in a man. But I disagree. God blessed me with a special dad, and I can see a lot of beauty in you.

Thank you, dear dad. Thank you for being. I love how your talents became my talents too!

Thankful for My Parents

Mom and Dad,

Thank you for bringing me into the world and for raising me well. Thank you for letting me go. Thank you for allowing me to start a new life across the Atlantic Ocean, and thank you for learning to live with this reality. Now as a parent, I am aware living far away from your child is a huge challenge. Thank you for allowing me to choose my life path. Thank you for all your support and love. Thank you for being mine.

God bless you, dear parents! I love you very much! My soul will always remember you as being beautiful and happy.

Thank you, thank you!

Thankful for My Marius

Darling, thank you for being my husband. Thank you for your unconditional love and support. Thank you for putting up with all my weirdness and all my imperfections.

Dear Marius, there is a precious picture taken at our fifteenth anniversary on the beach; we are down on our knees in front of each other. This photo depicts everything I feel and think of you. I am honored to be your wife.

When couples face difficulties, way too often they bail on marriage; they decide to go separate ways. I'm so grateful that challenges keep making us stronger and wiser. I'm so grateful to grow up—not just grow old—with you.

Dear Marius,

Choosing you as my forever partner was the best decision I ever made. Thank you for being a gorgeous light in my life.

God bless you, darling!

I love us!

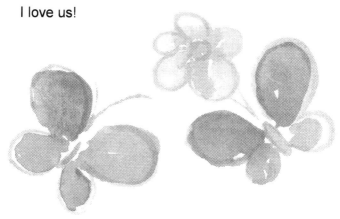

Thankful for My Favorite Tattoo on My Heart

David guides my plane to really high places,
to unexpected destinations.
One hour we are up in the clouds;
next hour we are down on the yucky mucky roads.

We are growing together,
we are learning together,
we are laughing and crying together.

Life is so beautiful but also so brutal at times!
I am grateful for my pilot.
Life got bigger, more intense,
way more beautiful, and much harder too.
This amazing human being showed up
to take me places I never dreamed I'd go!

Thank you, David! Thank you, my precious boy!

Thankful for Deep
Conversations with My David

Out of the blue, David asks me, "Is the word that means 'joy' in Romanian the same with the word that means 'love'?"

"No, there are two words: *bucurie* and *iubire*," I reply.

David continues, "What about 'happiness'?"

"Yes, there is a specific word for that too. It's *fericire*," I tell him.

David goes on, "What's the difference between happiness and joy?"

I explain to him, "Usually people expect some conditions to be met in order to be happy. Joy, on the other hand, is always inside us, even when we are sad, even when we don't feel too well, even when we are hungry or angry. We just have to uncover it and to release it."

David has a mini revelation. "So even when I'm doing homework, I still have joy inside me."

Me, smiling big, "Yes, joy is always inside us."

Grateful for My Brother's Family

Grateful for my dear, dear relatives overseas:
my big brother, Danilu, who
gives the best bear hugs
and jokes a lot.

My strong sister-in-law, Ruxi;
the two of us spent a couple of great days
in Lisbon in fall 2017,
bonding and exploring the city and its vicinity.

Luana, my beautiful niece,
a honeymoon child,
a sweet, talkative birdie.

Filip, my fierce warrior nephew,
a smart cookie,
a good soccer player.

I do not meet them
face-to-face often,
but they are always in my heart
and in my thoughts.

Grateful to have a sibling,
Grateful to have a "sister-in-love,"
Grateful for their children,
Grateful for our memories together!

Grateful for Children

Grateful for the tiny humans with big hearts.
Children are the most beautiful beings.

Blessed are the times when
I play like a child.

Since I was a little girl,
I knew I was going to
work with children,
so I do!

Children are the wisest;
they use all their gifts,
manifest pure joy,
show curiosity,
express spontaneity,
swim in freedom,
use blunt honesty,
stay—with no effort—in the present moment.

Children are my people, my tribe.
Children teach me a lot,
and my biggest teacher is my son.

We are all children,
God's precious kids.

Grateful for My Friends

My friends are the best. I have many beautifully talented friends. Some of my friends are gifted teachers. Some of my friends are good listeners. Some of my friends have the ability to fall and rise time and time again. Some of my friends cook the most delicious dishes. Some of my friends read and recommend amazing books. Some of my friends travel the world. Some of my friends give powerful yet gentle hugs. Some of my friends have a wicked sense of humor. Some of my friends chase their dreams every day. Some of my friends live closer and closer to the heart of things; they love to keep evolving.

I am so blessed with tons of awesome friends. I do not say or think "my best friend" anymore. Instead, I believe all my friends are the best. Each one of them owns special talents; each one of them shines a unique light. I have things to learn from all my friends. I genuinely appreciate them all.

Dear, Dear Friends,

I am thankful for the time spent with you, having fun together, exploring life side by side, and having heartfelt conversations with you. Thank you for being in my life!

Thankful for My Romanian Community

Let me tell you a true story. Listen …

It's a hot July afternoon. The sun adorns our backyard for yet another pool party. It's become a dear tradition for my family of friends.

David's excitement carries him around the pool. Not swimming, but walking in a fast pace. Marius jumps into the liquid paradise to cool his thoughts. He still gets a bit nervous when we have lots of guests. I do too. Nevertheless, we take a lot of pleasure in having friends over. Our pool acts like a huge magnet for our Romanian group.

All of a sudden, David triumphantly announces, "They are here!" Friends start pouring into our summer day. Lots of fun loving families: Barcan, Ursu, Tarau, Tiuca-Cojocariu, Soveja, Cretu, Verzes, Petrovan, Moldovan, Sandru, Avram. Daisy, our cat, scared of these intruders, escapes to the shed. Kids jump into the pool the second they say "Hello." Dads are eying the cool bottles of beer, while my girlfriends parade their happy summer dresses, and start talking all at once. The quiet from minutes ago evaporates, and a beautiful chaos starts its reign. Laughter mixes with splashes, a Latino song from my neighbor's yard comes like an uninvited but full-of-life guest, a child yells, and another tries to get everybody's attention to witness his new trampoline trick. The smells from the grill tickle our nostrils, and our bellies claim their shares. Each family has brought something tasty. Salads, sausages, corn on the cob, special appetizers, and homemade bread are all squeezed on the big table. My friend Camelia, the best baker in the universe, surprises me with my favorite coffee cake.

Kids stay for hours in the water. Their wet smiles are priceless. Just the thought of ice cream makes them take quick breaks. My David, an only child, looks so thrilled to have so many kids around. Marius and Gabi get piles of hot dogs and hamburgers ready. Some of my girlfriends are sunbathing while caressing cool margaritas. A strong dad—Alin—is throwing kid after kid in the air in the middle of the pool. I'd love to place their laughter into a treasure chest.

This concert of life takes everybody on an adventure for the whole afternoon. Our pool parties are sprinkled with glimpses of heaven: children's joy, parents' relaxed manner, clear skies, gorgeous flowers, yummy food, smiles galore.

My little family is surrounded by happiness. I am so thankful for pool parties in our backyard, so thankful for my family of friends!

Grateful for My Overseas Friends

Dear Overseas Friends,
There is no distance
that love cannot conquer.

Even though
we do not put our arms
around each other often,
our connection
gets stronger and stronger;
we are knit together for life!

Thank you,
my beautiful
overseas friends!
I miss you!
I love you very much!

Thankful for My Little Family

Before David goes to sleep, Marius and I join him in his bedroom for prayer time Adamut style. We count our blessings.

Giving thanks together as a family is one of the closest things to heaven I am experiencing here on earth. Not long ago, David came up with the idea of singing our thank-yous. One night he made up a rap song about his reasons of being grateful. It was so cool. I am sure God was enjoying it too. Last night he copied my singing; he was my echo.

I love these moments when we leave behind whatever the day brought us. The lights are out, the room gets quiet, and our inner lights are on. In the dark, we see more clearly the beauty of the day, the beauty of our lives. We are blessed, so very blessed. Thank you, God!

Dear Reader

Who are your people?
Who's your tribe?
Who lights up your soul?
How often do you show your love
in a way that's meaningful to them?

Call a dear one today.
Thank him/her for being in your life.
Be grateful for all the ways in which
he/she enhances your human experience.

Thank your mother, your father, your siblings.
Thank your kids, your husband/wife.
Give thanks to and for all your people.
They are precious to you.
Your appreciation will make their hearts smile.

CHAPTER 4

INSPIRATIONAL PEOPLE

Grateful for Artists

Grateful for artists'
unique visions,
marvelous creations,
abilities to express the deepest feelings,
aptitudes to imagine unbelievably beautiful worlds.
Grateful for all original, genial, creative people.

Grateful for art's
power to transport me to Wonderland,
invite to explore magical places and feelings,
capacity to guide me toward my inner-self,
potential to make me feel ageless.
Grateful for art daring me to fly.

Grateful for my favorite manifestations of creativity:
songs, stories, poems,
photographs, paintings, performances.

Grateful for my own artistic skills.
Grateful for being able
to birth the poems and the stories inside me,
to escape to a world of words,
to get lost in my imagination,
to free my spirit.

Grateful for Ioana Cretu

Your art sings on my walls,
a concert in every room.
My insomnia winks at your "Joy" sign.

Painting with your fingers,
touching lives even deeper.
Pouring acrylic paint in my heart's jars,
a swirl of colors tracing the path
from your essence to mine,
the same God in both of us.

Thinking of your soul spread
on canvases around the world,
abstract figures swaying
in earthy tones and rebel shapes.

Thank you, beautiful curly friend! Thank you for your
creativity and your shiny presence in my life.

(April 21, 2020)

Grateful for Oprah

Dear Oprah,

Thank you for helping, inspiring, and encouraging millions of people.

You changed my life by recommending the book *A New Earth: Awakening to Your Life's Purpose,* by Eckhart Tolle. This precious gift came into my life exactly when I was ready to get and live its message (spring 2014). I am on an amazingly beautiful life path because of this book, because of Eckhart Tolle, because of you. I am making new, much better choices now.

I am choosing to let my joy fly.
I am choosing to spread my light.
I am choosing to befriend my fears.
I am choosing to understand and accept my challenges.
I am choosing to believe I am bigger than my problems.
I am choosing to be present.
I am choosing to fully live this miracle called life.

Dear Oprah,

I would love to give you the biggest thank you hug. I am dreaming of you reading my book one day. Grateful for you!

Grateful for Teachers

Teachers do one of the hardest but
one of the most important and
most beautiful jobs ever!

Grateful for my boy's teachers!
Thank you for your kindness and
your endless patience.
Thank you for making David feel
appreciated for what he already is
while encouraging him
to reach his potential,
to become the best version of himself.

Grateful for all my teacher friends;
we are one awesome family.

"Let us remember: One book, one pen, one child, one
teacher can change the world" (Malala Yousafzai).

Grateful for Laurie Ventura

Thank you, my beautiful teacher friend,
for your sweet gesture
of saying yes right away
to a brand-new endeavor.
Thank you
for helping me edit my paper child.
I am grateful.

Thank you for your good suggestions,
your encouraging words,
and your hearts drawn on my pages.
I am grateful.

Thank you, dear Laurie,
for walking and talking together
on various paths of life.
I am grateful.

Grateful for Special Education Teachers

I have a deep admiration and respect for all born to be teachers. But thinking, writing, or talking about teachers working with special needs children is making my heart bow its head.

I am grateful for all the professionals working with children: teacher assistants, therapists, counselors, principals, doctors, behaviorists, psychologists. In my mind, you are all angels because all of you are constantly offering support and guidance to special students.

I see every one of you; I see you all doing this challenging job. I see you sharing in the joy of each tiny progress made by a student.

Thank you for each time a student believes you get him/her. Thank you for each time you speak a student's unique language.

Words are not able to express my gratitude for all teachers working with special needs children. I honestly believe you are handpicked by God. I would love to give each one of you a huge hug and to say, "Thank you," while looking into your light-filled eyes.

Dear Special Education Teachers,

May life give you as many beautiful surprises in return for the many hours you spend guiding these little souls. Thank you for your endless patience, love, and dedication.

Grateful for Tina Sosna

Some people are close to my heart even though I've never met them. Such people enrich my life, inspire me, and offer me plenty of moments of pure bliss. These special persons are hungry for beauty, and they know how to use their gifts.

Tina Sosna radiates light. She is a very creative artist who connects with nature in a delicate manner, and this fascinates me. The thing that captivates me the most about Tina is her ability to find extraordinary details in ordinary things and experiences.

Sometimes we are too caught up in our frenetic lives, and we overlook or ignore the magic that surrounds us. We've become blind to the beauty of the simple things.

Thanks to Tina, I pay more attention to the shadows. I rest my eyes more often on areas bathed in light. I take notice of a room corner caressed by the sunlight or of the playful trees' shadows winking at me. Things that may seem small to others mean a lot to me. They bring me tremendous joy!

Whenever I notice something beautiful while walking in the park, I think, *Thank you, Tina. Thank you for showing me how to feel the grass' heartbeats, the flowers' whispers, and the tree branches' ballerina-like movements. Thank you, Tina, for nudging me to be more present in nature.*

Sweet Tina,

Thank you for touching my soul. I am grateful for the way your light dances in the world! Keep shining bright!

Ode to Tree Shadows

Shapes dancing in the middle of the road,
My car swallows them whole.

Patterns growing, shrinking,
Ever-changing figures that hypnotize me.
Mysterious ghosts
Making me dreamy.

Stories written on the side
of the buildings and on the pavement.

You are gentle friends feeding my imagination
every sunny, windy day.

You call my name
from another world.
And I always answer.

Grateful for Don

Sometimes, if you are lucky enough, you meet a special person who takes your breath away. People like this have a unique aura. Their light shines bright, and their hearts are as big as the sky. They live by serving others. Isn't this the best way to show your love?

A person like this is Don. I am so honored to have had the chance to cross paths with this soul, this gentleman. I do not know much about Don's private life, but I can tell you this: He is an angel.

One may say that Don was a one man show at Good News Christian Preschool in Keyport, where I used to work. One day he was Santa, talking gently with the kids settled comfortably on his lap. Another day he was farmer Don who came and explained to the children about growing and harvesting vegetables and fruits. Yet another day, he was making possible the Mr. Skip's music show. And another blessed day, he brought yummy, homemade cross buns for teachers.

If only you could have seen Don at his ninetieth birthday party, when everyone was wearing his favorite color, red.

Don is always wearing a big warm smile on his face. He looks like a grandpa who is everybody's favorite person. The grandpa who is always ready to offer a hug and ready to read you a good story by the fire. Don is a kind person who acts like Santa all year around. He looks a lot like Santa too.

I have a special place in my heart for elderly people who inspire me. Ninety-two-year-old Don is probably on top of my list. God bless you, Don! Thank you for inspiring me.

My Book's Angel

My gratitude book would have not been possible without Tara Verzella. She is a friend of a friend. We are Facebook friends, and we met a couple of times at our mutual friend's celebratory events.

In November 2018, a beautiful idea came to me. Each day of the month I would post on Facebook something I am grateful for. I also attached a picture to my posts, an image reflecting that special something that lifts me up.

Sweet Tara left me a kind and thoughtful comment suggesting I gather all these "Thank you for something" posts in a gratitude book. What a wonderful idea! For the first time ever, I knew my love of words and my joy of being will turn into something very special. That's how *Grateful* was called into the world.

I can't ever thank Tara enough for guiding me toward this beautiful dream of mine. I wasn't aware of having this strong desire in my heart to write a book, but when Tara made her suggestion, it felt so right that I came to believe this dream was inside me for a long time.

Thank you, Tara, for writing your thoughts about my gratitude posts. Your simple, pure act means a lot to me. I just needed a nudge. I just needed a reminder to use my wings and to fly high.

Tara, God bless your amazing heart! You are one of my angels! I hope an angel will guide you as well in fulfilling one of your dearest dreams.

God is smiling.
You did well.
We did well.

Grateful for All the People Who Inspire Me

I am inspired by people who are chasing their dreams every single day.

I am inspired by people who are not afraid to be deeply touched by life.

I am inspired by families with lots of children, by their naturalness and easiness.

I am inspired by people who sing, even if they sing badly.

I am inspired by people who dance with or without rhythm.

I am inspired by people who still smile when dark clouds cover the skies of their lives.

I am inspired by people who do not give too much thought to what's fashionable.

I am inspired by people who follow their hearts and intuitions.

I am inspired by people who are not afraid to say no while saying it in a loving way.

I am inspired by people who go to sleep saying, "Thank you for another day lived well."

I am inspired by people who are honest with themselves.

I am inspired by people who honor themselves and treat themselves nicely.

I am inspired by people who treat others with great care and love.

I am inspired by people who are brave to share their life stories.

I am inspired by people who understand the simple truths of life, and

I am inspired by people who live simple lives themselves.

I am inspired by people who try their best to understand and accept all others.

I am inspired by people who know they are worthy, valuable, and lovable.

I am inspired by people who admit their mistakes.

I am inspired by people who learn from their failures.

I am inspired by people who are confident and humble at the same time.

I am inspired by people who are playful regardless of their ages.

I am inspired by passionate people.

I am inspired by people who make time for their hobbies.

I am inspired by people who never get bored.

I am inspired by married couples who still go on dates.

I am inspired by people who know how to enjoy their own company.

I am inspired by people who love being in nature.

I am inspired by people who are dedicated to animals.

I am inspired by people who respect everything that is alive.

I am inspired by people who show kindness to everyone.

I am inspired by caring neighbors, like mine.

I am inspired by people who give freely and gladly, no expectations attached.

I am inspired by people who know that the mind needs to bow to the heart.

I am inspired by people who collect experiences, not possessions.

I am inspired by people who have patience, so they were able to finish reading this.

Thank you!

Dear Reader

Who inspires you?
Who gives you wings to reach the stars
and touch your dreams?

Who are the people
you'd like to meet one day
to tell them, "Thank you for
improving my life and the world"?

Can you write them a letter or an e-mail?
Can you send them your love, your good vibes?
Can you keep them in your best thoughts and in your
prayers?

Think of the people who inspire you.
Please whisper, "Thank you for inspiring me.
Thank you for sharing your light."

CHAPTER 5

PIECES OF ME

Grateful for My Body

Thank you heart. You are my favorite engine. You are my favorite muscle. You are tirelessly pumping blood throughout my body. How can I ever thank you enough?

Thank you eyes for helping me see and discover so many treasures: my dear ones, fall's colors, the food I'm eating, the maple tree in front of my house, the road I'm driving on, the pages of the books that allow me to travel to unimaginable places.

Thank you hands and arms for helping me write my gratitude book, caress my boys, wash dishes, pick flowers, swim in the ocean, cuddle my dear ones, touch velvety petals. Thankful for being able to hold hands with my darling.

Thank you brain for helping me remember, learn, think, make connections, solve problems. Thankful for my right side of the brain, the center of my creativity, intuition, imagination, music, and art awareness!

Thank you feet for helping me walk every day to the bathroom and to the kitchen, to school and back, to faraway lands. Dear feet, thank you for helping me run, dance, and tiptoe.

Thank you internal organs. You are functioning for me every single second. I can go to sleep, and you still continue your work. You are awesome.

Thank you muscles, thank you tissues, thank you

skin, thank you bones, thank you cells, thank you saliva, thank you nails.

Thank you nose for helping me enjoy the smell of a freshly baked bread, the crisp smell of a winter day, David's baby-like smell that still lingers around his neck.

Thank you ears for helping me savor music, for helping me hear my own whisper, for helping me hear my family's and friends' words. Thank you ears for allowing me to enjoy the birds' and the wind's songs. Thank you ears for making it possible to hear my mama's voice on the phone from across the ocean.

Thank you mouth for helping me talk, sing, kiss, eat, smile, and blow in the hot bowl of soup. Thank you mouth for the blessed times you just rest and leave the silence do all the talking.

Thank you body, you are a piece of art. You are whole, you are perfect, you are an intricate container of my spirit. Thank you for being.

Grateful for My Soul

My soul:
a huge city with soft boulevards and song rivers;
a subway, and at every station more miracles jump in;
a child climbing a sunray;
an invitation to stay present.

My soul:
an open window,
an endless ocean,
a phoenix bird,
a colorful dream.

My soul:
a river in love with its journey,
the rocks washed by the river,
the riverbed,
and the eye of the one calling it "river."

My soul:
a fresh slice of bread,
the bread of life.
Are you hungry?
Have a piece of my soul.

Grateful for My Imperfections

I do have so many.
I choose to work on my imperfections
with lots of love and kindness.
I choose not to put myself down.

I treasure my imperfections.
They make me human;
they teach me humility,
tolerance, and compassion.

Working on my imperfections
opens my eyes and
enlarges my heart.

I am so grateful for being
an imperfectly perfect human being!

Grateful for My Gifts

I am shining bright.
You see my aura.
I am pointing out the source of my light.
You understand.

Our gifts are precious.
Our gifts are unique.
Our gifts don't belong to us.
Our gifts are coming through us.

We are the vessels of our gifts.
Blessed, very blessed vessels.

Thank you, God,
for trusting me with
such beautiful gifts!

Grateful for Being an Extrovert and an Introvert

Grateful for having the best of both worlds; I am an extrovert and an introvert.

I enjoy spending time with good friends talking, laughing, sharing, and building precious memories. I declare myself a part-time social butterfly.

I am also very fond of "me time." As I grow older and wiser, I'm learning to appreciate more and more my own company. I am the most important person in my life. Just by honoring myself, I am able to honor others as well. Many times I look forward to spending quality time by myself. Love the moments when I am able to relax, create, get inspired, reflect, or just notice the beauty of the world. I may be alone, but I never feel lonely.

What about you? Are you an extrovert or an introvert?

Grateful for My Most Memorable Encounters

In my twenties I met my husband.
In my thirties I met my child.
In my forties I met my… self.

What an amazing life journey so far!

Grateful for My Silliness

Grateful for laughter,
grateful for my good sense of humor.

Don't take yourself too seriously!
Unhook your bra or
unbuckle your pants,
take a deep breath,
get loose,
get your crazies out.

Dance like an army of fleas attacked you.
Smile like the sun is trapped inside you.
Grab somebody, and give them the biggest hug ever,
or wrap your arms around yourself, and
give yourself a huge hug.

Be silly today; relax.
Pour yourself a drink of joy elixir, and
see what happens.

Dear Reader

Give thanks for your body,
for the parts you think are great,
for the parts you find okay, and
for the parts you think are not good enough.
Give thanks for all of you.

Give thanks for your soul,
for your spirit,
for your beauty,
for your mind,
for your heart,
for your patience,
for your creativity,
for your dedication,
for your compassion,
for your tolerance,
for your bravery.
Give thanks for all of you.

Give thanks for your desire to better yourself.
Give thanks for all your ups and downs.
Give thanks for your whole life journey.
Give thanks for all of you.

CHAPTER 6

MESSY BEAUTIFUL LIFE

Her Story

She lived in fear,
barely making it from
the sunup to the moonrise.

Angst walked in her veins;
her own shadow was afraid of
breaking her.

She smelled like dread.
Her thoughts,
crumbs for darkness.

She lived in this cold pit,
and one gray day,
fear claimed her.

Swiftly, she woke up
and snapped.
Fear recoiled and dropped dead.

In the woman's chest,
a butterfly dried its wings
and escaped.

A Reminder

I would love to share with you
more about my journey with my son.

The persons I admire most
are those who can openly talk about their struggles,
about their life lessons,
about the pains of growing wings.

I am in awe of authentic people.
Also, being open about my trials with my son
could benefit others who have similar challenges.

But these things do not matter as much as this fact:
I've come to realize this is not my story to tell.
It's David's story.
I have to respect that.

A reminder: I am full of joy, nevertheless
I have a full basket of hard moments too.
I am like everybody else.
And I've learned to love my messy beautiful life!

Grateful for Wake-Up Calls

This season I let fear take me in its arms.
I let anxiety crumple my heart.
I let the feeling of not knowing drive me crazy.
I let my boys see me sad or in distress way too often.

I am craving peace.
I need spring to bloom inside me.
I am ready to reclaim my joy.

Life is hard sometimes,
but I am not done fighting.
I just lost sight of the light for a while.

Life is offering me a new chance to grow.
She's saying, "Alina, are you ready for more growing?"
And honestly, how can I say no
when growing is what life is all about?

(February 2019)

P. S. Strong people are
not afraid to
show their vulnerable parts.

Even though I am on a
new life path now,
challenges and wake-up calls
frequently meet me in unexpected places.

Let's Always Give Thanks

Let's give thanks when life feels heavy.

Let's give thanks when the present moment hurts.

Let's give thanks when anxious thoughts grab us with a hundred tight arms.

Let's give thanks when the idea of not knowing the future drives us crazy.

Let's give thanks when our breath is short and rushed.

Let's give thanks when tears talk about our pain.

Let's give thanks when life feels like a mocked version of our dreams.

Let's give thanks when we are frustrated.

Let's give thanks when we cannot control a certain outcome.

Let's give thanks when the sun is stubbornly hiding from view.

Let's give thanks when we make mistakes or when others wrong us.

Let's give thanks daily, no matter what!

Yes

Yes, I have battles to fight.
Yes, my life is not easy.
Yes, I still have doubts.
Yes, challenges visit me often.
Yes, sometimes I don't have the answer.
Yes, some hours are heavy, so heavy.
Yes, I still am anxious at times.
Yes, I still have fears.

Yes, my life path is filled with blessings.
Yes, I find beauty everywhere and in everyone.
Yes, I made peace with life.
Yes, I am cocreating my journey.
Yes, I am brave enough.
Yes, I go to sleep with a smile inside me.
Yes, I always carry the light within me.
Yes, my heart is full of joy.
Yes, my love is bigger than my fears.
Big yes!

Thankful for Being Bigger
than My Challenges

A while ago I read something beautiful, something that goes along these lines:

The circumstances of our lives are like waves in the ocean. Sometimes our waves are bigger, higher, crazier than usual. Other times our waves are softer, fewer, or almost imperceptible. We are not our waves. We are the ocean! The ocean is always still. The ocean is not bothered by its waves. The ocean goes much deeper and much farther than its waves.

Seek deeper. Search farther. Look for that special place inside you that defines you. Look for one "thing" that will not change depending on the circumstances of your life. Go beyond the waves, beyond the appearances.

For a long time, I was lost in the middle of the ocean. For a long time, I allowed the waves to define my life.

So many crazy waves still come into my life. So many times I am still surprised or crushed by the power of a wave, but every single time, I am coming back home. I am coming back to the place where all is calm and quiet.

I am the ocean!

Dear Reader

What hurtful experience
later brought good into your life?

What painful memory
helped you grow as a person?

What "knife in the heart" experience
led you to wisdom and courage?

Can you see it as a passed exam,
as a needed step on your way to greatness?

Give thanks for all that's good in your life,
but most important, learn to
give thanks for challenges.
Obstacles are here to take you and me
to the other side!

CHAPTER 7

LIFE LESSONS

Grateful for Being Enough

I am beautiful enough.
I am smart enough.
I am brave enough.
I am trendy enough.
I am sweet enough.
I am efficient enough.
I am crazy enough.
I am happy enough.
I am amazing enough.
I am friendly enough.
I am helpful enough.
I am compassionate enough.
I am enough in every possible way.
I am enough.
I am more than enough.
I am still becoming!

Grateful for Finding My Home

My belief is that home
is not an external place
but an internal one.

Home is making peace with ourselves.
Home is a state of mind.
Home means resting comfortably in our lives,
in our hearts.

Grateful,
so grateful
for finding my home!

Grateful for Being Okay with Not Being Okay

It's okay sometimes not to know what to do.
It's okay sometimes to screw it up.
It's okay sometimes to lose it.
It's okay sometimes to feel pain.
It's okay sometimes to cry rivers.
It's okay sometimes to make mistakes.
It's okay sometimes to feel like running away.
It's okay sometimes not to know what to say.
It's okay sometimes to say the wrong thing.
It's okay sometimes to be messy.
It's okay sometimes to be in ego's grip.
It's okay sometimes to fail.
It's okay sometimes to yell.
It's okay sometimes to throw a tantrum.
It's okay sometimes to wanna be left alone.
It's okay sometimes to suffer.
It's okay sometimes not to feel good enough.
It's okay not to be okay.

Let's do one day at a time, one hour at a time,
one minute at the time. It's okay!

Thankful for Welcoming Change

"You've changed."

When people told me this in the past, I used to be somehow hurt by it. Hearing these words used to make me sad. My interpretation was, "I used to be good, and now I'm not." Being told I've changed made me question myself. Not anymore.

We are meant to grow. We are meant to change. We are not the same as we were yesterday, and this is great news. We are evolving. We are becoming what we are meant to be!

Please keep changing. Please go with the flow. Pretty please, do not stay stuck in old patterns, old ideas, and preconceptions. Be flexible. Be open. Learn. Let life take you on unexpected adventures.

Next time when someone tells you, "You changed," you can answer, "I really hope so!" or, "Thank you. That's exactly what I've been aiming for" (Maya Shetreat).

Grateful for Recognizing My Power

I am grateful for being able to do hard things.

Getting through challenging seasons, weeks, hours.
Going to sleep with a smile in my heart even if it rains.
Remembering tomorrow will bring a new chance.

I am grateful for being able to do hard things.

Keeping sight of the light during troubled times,
Knowing life is a perfect blend of pain and joy.
Learning to accept everything that comes my way.

I am grateful for being able to do hard things.

Thankful for Being Whole

For most of my life I saw myself as a half,
always expecting something or
someone to complete me.

When I got married,
I called my husband "my better half."
I actually declared myself a lower-quality half.

Then I woke up, and
I smiled big because
I saw the truth.

It is so empowering to know we are complete.
Nothing is missing, nothing can be added.

What a liberating feeling.
I am whole!

Grateful for Learning to Fill My Own Bucket

I do not wait for the world,
for my boy,
for my husband, or friends to
make me happy.
This is my responsibility!

I am becoming an expert in making myself feel
loved,
appreciated,
beautiful,
valuable.
It's an inside job!

I am filling my own bucket.
All the love that comes my way
is just a bonus, an awesome bonus.

Thankful for Possibilities

We tend to say:
"This is good,"
"That is bad,"
"This is right,"
"That is wrong."

We tend to look at things or people
in a narrow-minded way,
thinking a situation is
either black or white,
thinking we reached
either the rock bottom or the highest peak.
But in reality, the options are endless.

Believe in abundance.
See more than two possibilities.

This wisdom bit
is often inviting me to expand my horizons,
to make room in my mind and in my heart
for the unknown,
to learn seeing outside the box,
to visualize the complexity of the possible outcomes.

Grateful for the countless ways
abundance shows up in my life!

Dear Reader

Please repeat each statement below. After each one, pause for a minute and reflect. Let their meaning sink inside you. Open your mind and your heart to their truths. If it's possible, please say the words out loud. Try to smile. Thank you!

I am beautiful enough.
I am smart enough.
I am brave enough.
I am trendy enough.
I am sweet enough.
I am efficient enough.
I am amazing enough.
I am friendly enough.
I am helpful enough.
I am compassionate enough.
I am crazy enough.
I am good enough.
I am enough.
I am more than enough.
I am still becoming.

CHAPTER 8

UNLIKELY THANK-YOUS

Grateful for Soul Pain

I know it sounds crazy,
but my experience taught
me suffering can open
the gate to many blessings.

I am grateful for the pain
that helped me grow.
I'm grateful for the pain
that helped me become a wiser,
kinder human being.

I am so grateful
I was given the chance to transform
the lowest point of my life into
a beautiful new path.

Some years ago,
I got overwhelmed by my life circumstances.
I felt completely lost.
I saw myself as inadequate,
not a good enough mother,
not a good enough daughter,
not a good enough friend,
not a good enough wife,
not a good enough person.

At the same time,
I was so ready for
a shift in my life.

My journey from a worrier to a warrior
is one of the most amazing and humbling
experiences ever.

I will always treasure the huge gift
pain gave me.
I am so grateful for my new life,
my new perspective,
my freedom.

Grateful for Beautiful Strangers

On our way to the Grand Canyon, we stopped at a scenic viewpoint. I got out of the car and noticed two couples, one in their sixties and the other one closer to eighties. The younger woman asked for a hug from the older lady as they were about to part ways. They wished each other well. The older gentleman gathered the four of them in a circle and started praying. He thanked God for the beautiful places they all visit and for his everlasting love and protection. I was so touched by this scene, so I approached them saying, "That was so beautiful, the four of you praying together. I want to give you all a hug, a group hug."

We hugged and talked a bit. I told them about my beautiful home country, Romania, and about the gratitude book I am writing. The older gentleman shared a nice little story. He said he often prays spontaneously with people he just met. One time he exited Home Depot and heard a lady telling another lady, "I'm going to pray for this." He interfered, "What are you going to pray for?" The ladies told him, and the three of them started praying right there in front of the store.

This memory of four strangers praying outdoors will stay with me. Four strangers praying together in the middle of wilderness.

I am so grateful for meeting these people. I am

so grateful for moments like this. Moments when God makes it possible for me to cross paths with angels. Thankful for moments when life surprises me, moments when I feel connected with all people.

I am so grateful for beautiful strangers.

Grateful for the In-Between Moments

Getting ready for school,
Doing chores,
Washing away the dirt,
Refreshing the water in a flower vase
Waiting for the bus,
The last hour of work before the day is over,
The soup is almost done,
Walking to a meeting place,
Setting the table,
Cleaning the dishes,
Preparing the class,
Doing research for a new treatment,
Wiping away tears,
Cutting cuticles,
Getting ready for taking a photo.

Grateful for the in-between moments.
Let's not overlook them.
Let's treasure them.
They are a big part of our lives!

Grateful for Mind Striptease

Strip off the layers of beliefs that make you think
you are not fit enough, beautiful enough,
creative enough, smart enough.

Strip off the layers of beliefs that make you think
your child is here to make you happy,
to fulfill your expectations.

Strip off the layers of beliefs that make you think
your partner, your family, and your friends are here
to make you feel loved and special.

Strip off the layers of beliefs that make you think
you are a victim
of your life's circumstances.

Strip off the layers of beliefs that make you think
your job, your hobbies, your possessions
are what give you worth.

Strip off the layers of beliefs that make you think
your bank account and your health insurance
bring you safety and protection.

Strip off the layers of beliefs that make you think
the labels placed on you by yourself or others
define you.

Strip off the layers of beliefs that make you think
too much about pleasing others;
you end up betraying yourself.

Strip off the layers of beliefs that make you think
you are a separate entity,
that you are not an essential part of the whole.

Strip off the layers of
yesterday's regrets and
tomorrow's worries.

Strip off the layers you built
to protect yourself from
life's blows.

Strip off the last layers of
whatever you constructed with your mind,
in your mind.

Now you are sitting naked
in front of the mirror,
a mirror that does not show a body
but the whole you.

Look at yourself; take your time.
This is the sexiest version of you.
The most attractive one.
The most beautiful one.
The most accurate one.
The humblest and the most confident one.
The purest one.
The only one that's really you.
The only one that life intended for you,
for me, for everybody.

Own the naked you!
Own your truth!
You are perfect!

Grateful for Mondays

Mondays have a bad reputation. Most people do not like them very much. One recent Monday, while driving David to school, I heard him complaining about this "awful day." A nice idea came to me. I said, "Let's play a game. Let's find as many scenarios as possible when Monday can be a great day."

Monday is a great day when it's your child's birthday.
Monday is a great day when one gets some good news.
Monday is a great day if we spend some time doing what we love most.
Monday is a great day when we read a good book.
Monday is a great day when we eat something delicious.
Monday is a great day when you do something silly.
Monday is a great day if you wear mismatched socks.
Monday is great day if the sun unexpectedly shows up.
Monday is a great day when you are on vacation.
Monday is a great day if you leave that day for a trip.
Monday is a great day when a new experience starts on that day.
Monday is a great day when you do a nice thing for somebody who is not feeling well.
Monday is a great day when somebody surprises you with a little something.

Monday is a great day when you don't have to go to work or to school.
Monday is a great day when you see signs of a new season you love.
Monday is a great day if you start it by smiling or listening to your favorite song.

Monday is great day when we wake up and
decide to live it well.
Monday, like any other day,
is a gift, a blessing.

Unlikely Thank-Yous

Thankful for toilet paper.
Thankful for garbage cans.
Thankful for tampons.
Thankful for tissues.
Thankful for nail clippers.
Thankful for wipes.
Thankful for brooms.
Thankful for road signs.
Thankful for snowplows.
Thankful for sieves.
Thankful for bags.
Thankful for windows.
Thankful for recipes.
Thankful for silverware.
Thankful for bedsheets.
Thankful for carpets.
Thankful for notepads.
Thankful for pens.
Thankful for staplers.

Thankful for a billion useful things
we take for granted.

Thanks to all the creative minds
who invent cool and
practical things that make
our lives easier.

Dear Reader

Can you think of one object
in your household or in your neighborhood,
one item that seems insignificant,
something that one would never think to give thanks for?
Something like wire fences or doorknobs.
Something that has a practical use,
still we take that certain something for granted?

Please find five objects you take for granted.
Give thanks for them.
These things are helping our lives
more than we give them credit for.

Say "Thank you … for easing our lives.
Thank you to the inventors who brought you to life."

CHAPTER 9

SIMPLE PLEASURES OF LIFE

My darling David is the author of this chapter's title.

Grateful for Books

Some of my best friends have pages.
Through their thousand eyes
I see the whole universe and
many new worlds.

A precious hour
surprises my family
in the same bed,
each one of us reading our own books.
Daisy creates a cozy nest for herself
among our warm limbs,
completing our perfect family portrait.

I am grateful for my family's passion for words,
both written and spoken words.

I am grateful for Barnes & Noble,
our favorite bookstore,
that greets us often.

I am grateful for local libraries;
we exit them holding armfuls of books.

I am grateful for being part of two book clubs;
one meets online, one gathers us around a table.

I am grateful for audio books;
almost always a story is "on" in our house.

I am grateful for our red box in front of our house,
our Little Free Library.
It invites people who walk or drive by
to grab a book and to leave a book.

Some of my best friends have pages.
We talk to each other for hours
after the last page was left behind.

Grateful for the infinite beautiful worlds
contained inside books.

Grateful for Music

Love listening to meditation music while writing.
Love listening to rock and roll while dancing.
Love listening to Alicia Keys
when my soul needs a ride on the swings.

Love listening to nature's music.
Love listening to silence's songs.

Grateful for songwriters who
translate raw emotions into beautiful songs.
Grateful for tunes that
take me places I've never been to.
Grateful for children's songs that
remind me who I am.

Love going to concerts.
Love sharing the live experience.
Love filling up with music's energy and power.
Love being hugged by the same songs
like thousands of other fans.

Grateful for my musician friends who
surprise my heart time and again.
Christiana, you were born inside a musical note,
and now you are bigger than a jazz song.
Johanna, you rock my world
in the best possible way.

Grateful for the magical gift of music.
Grateful for music's unforgettable touch.

Grateful for Dance

"Dance like nobody's watching" (Susannah Clark).

Moving my body
to music's vibes.
The older I get,
the freer I feel.

Dance, an irresistible
invitation to
escape time
and the material world.

Dance, a beautiful
manifestation of our light,
a way to express our joy,
our freedom,
our energy.

"Dance for All of Us, Alina"

Out of my skin,
Immune to my surroundings,
Time and space melt,
All desires abandoned.
Being totally here,
Inside a song.

Exiting the narrow streets of the mind,
Strolling through freedom woods.
Embracing a bird tree,
Smelling a sunray,
Tasting the liquid air,
Throwing my limbs in the wind,
Allowing my heart to scream.

Yes, dear Darlene, today I'm dancing for all of us!

Grateful for Handwritten Letters

In times of digital supremacy,
my pen pal Anca and I
love to use ink and patience
to get to each other.

Even though she lives
just a couple of towns away,
old souls communicate better
on paper.

I treasure the hours when
I write or read a handwritten letter.

We tell stories about our storms and rainbows.
I stroll through her soul's jungle.
She rests on a bench in my heart.

So grateful for words that fly my way,
words telling me about your world, dear Anca.

Grateful for handwritten letters, handwritten dreams.

Grateful for Photographers

"Photograph: a picture painted by the sun without instruction in art" (Ambrose Bierce).

Hours and hours
contemplating delightful
pictures taken by
friends I haven't yet met.
Photographers
telling me stories,
oiling my insides with honey,
inviting me to peek into countless windows of heaven,
giving me the opportunity to collect light,
inspiring me to color my days in brighter tones,
making me feel privileged to see
the beauty of their worlds!

Thank you, dear photographers!

Grateful for TV Comedy Shows

Most nights Marius and I
watch a funny episode from a comedy show.
Just the right thing
to make us smile before sleep.

Our friends keep recommending thrillers or dramas.
"No, thanks," I say,
"our life's crazy enough.
We wanna relax and stay loose."

Seinfeld, Friends, Big Bang Theory,
Frasier, Everybody Loves Raymond
spread much lightness on our bed
and into our souls
moments before "Good nights"
are shared and pillows go to sleep.

Thank you, comedy shows.
You crack us up!

Looking Deeply

Sometimes
I see my cat, Daisy,
like never before.

Sometimes
I take my time noticing her whiskers,
her shiny white fur,
the texture of her brown spots.

Sometimes
my fingers get lost
in her softest fur,
that on her belly.

Sometimes
we lock eyes;
a spontaneous staring contest
takes places and
she almost always wins.

Sometimes
I study Daisy's tail movements;
she writes secret messages in the air.
Her tail can do magic tricks.
It becomes
a passionate conductor's arm,
a confident brush busy at work,
an exotic dancer.

Sometimes
I look beyond her small body.
I feel her spirit.
I understand we are one.

Sometimes
I am looking deeply.
So grateful for these simple,
powerful moments.

Grateful for the Joy of Being

Grateful for the precious moments
when we realize life is perfect
just the way it is,
moments when we tell ourselves,
"This is as good as it gets."

Heavenly moments are
hidden inside ordinary days.
Simple pleasures.
The simple pleasures of life.
The joy of being.

Dear Reader

What are your simple pleasures?
What are your guilty pleasures?
Give thanks for them today.

Don't worry they are not noble enough.
Say, "Thank you for being a part of my life."

Give thanks for online window-shopping.
Give thanks for soap operas.
Give thanks for listening on repeat to a certain song.
Give thanks for big containers of ice cream.

Give thanks for the little things that help you relax at
the end of a long, busy, tiring day or week.

Appreciate your favorite little indulgences.
Give thanks for them.
They are your friends who don't expect much in return,
just some quality time spent in your company.

CHAPTER 10

EXTRAORDINARY DAYS

Grateful for Glimpses of Heaven

Lying down on the beach with eyes closed,
Sinking in the sun's warm palms,
Allowing the ocean's music to cuddle our souls.

Being surprised by the beauty of the first snow.
Enjoying the fall colors: a yellow, orange, brown, and red dream.
Staying in the middle of a wildflower field, the wind gently moving the world.

Seeing the face of a newborn for the very first time.
Crying joy tears.
Being aware of God's presence in our lives.

Noticing two elderly people holding hands.
Witnessing people who go out of their way to help others in very challenging times.

Showing to the world our bright lights.
Seeing someone else share an inner gift.
Embracing who and what we are.
Feeling a rainbow of good feelings inside our hearts.

Grateful for glimpses of forever.
Grateful for glimpses of heaven.

Holding David for the First Time

Top of my list
of special days
is David's arrival.

My son was born on a cold December day.
Still, the warmest day of my heart.

Seeing his sweet face for the very first time,
marveling at his long black hair,
noticing his perfect … everything,
felt like miracles were raining on me.

What a blessed day!
Finally meeting David,
my biggest dream come true—
holding heaven in my arms.
Joy exploding like fireworks inside me.
Tasting eternity while still on earth.

Grateful for Trips

Packing and going places,
exploring the wide, wild world.
What a tremendous adventure!

I got the traveler bug,
the itch of discovering new
countries, cities, and national parks.
Novel corners of Eden.

I love all of it:
daydreaming before and after the trip,
anticipating the coming trip,
enjoying the days spent on the trip,
creating memories, and later on,
reliving the experiences through storytelling and
looking through the pictures time and again.

If somebody wakes me up
in the middle of the night and tells me,
"Alina, pack luggage for the whole family.
You are going on a trip in thirty minutes,"

I promise you,
I'll do it in less than half an hour, and
I'll be smiling the whole time.

Being a millionaire in trip memories
makes my smile
pack its own luggage and
fly.

"We travel not to escape life,
but for life not to escape us" (Anonymous).

Grateful for Poems Born on Trips

Countless treasures go camping
in my heart.
A sky full of wonders
nests in my soul.
Nature fills me
with beautiful gifts.

I may be skinny in body,
but my inner being stretches for
miles and miles and miles.
I'm fat with immaterial riches.

I'm obese with blessings!
I would never go on a diet.
On the contrary,
I plan to be the heaviest I can be ... on the inside.

(Page, Arizona, July 2019)

The Fifteenth Wedding Anniversary

I am not crazy about yellow-gold anymore,
so in 2016 I made the decision
to switch to white gold.

I envisioned my
fifteenth wedding anniversary like this:
Marius and I exchanging new rings, and
David witnessing this special ceremony and
being our ring bearer.

My dream came true.
One early July morning at Sandy Hook beach,
all three of us in white outfits,
me wearing a multicolor rose crown and
my heart in my eyes.

A perfect day.
The bluest sky caressing the sand and the ocean,
the sun blessing us with its smile.

David running to give us the rings.
Me crying while reading something
I wrote for the occasion.
Marius saying yes to all of this.

A precious hour,
moments to remember in ten lifetimes.
No words can express my gratitude
for that summer day's gifts.

Grateful for My Joy Festival

Every spring I gather girls outdoors
to celebrate life together,
to celebrate it with flowers.

We create flower crowns, and
sweet Neli teaches us how to make
amazing flower arrangements.

I call this get-together in nature Joy Festival,
one of my favorite days of the year.

We bring fruits and have a picnic too.
The little girls run around.
I do too, while proudly wearing my flower crown.

Connecting flowers,
connecting with nature,
connecting to each other.

Spring is a splendid song
I often daydream about.

Mother's Day at Longwood Gardens

I didn't know I had it in me,
but now I thoroughly believe it:
I am a designer.

What do I design?
My life.
How?

Like this:
I love, love, love Longwood Gardens in Pennsylvania.
About six years ago I told my boys
to take me there for Mother's Day.

That was the beginning of
a beautiful tradition.
We go once a year to the gardens,
in springtime,
my gift.

I would love to take all the women in my life there,
especially my cousin Dora,
my May flower girl.

Every single time
I visit Longwood Gardens,
millions of flowers
grab my heart,
tell me delightful stories,
give me unforgettable memories,
place lots of smiles on my lips,
stir up my joy,
make me feel grateful for being alive.

In Longwood Gardens I get drunk on beauty!

"Seeing beauty in a flower could awaken humans,
however briefly, to the beauty that is an essential
part of their own innermost being, their true nature"
(Eckart Tolle).

Dear Reader

What are the events,
what are the exceptional days,
what are the peaks of your life?

The day you got a promotion?
The day your darling first told you, "I love you"?
The day your kids were born?

Remember these precious days.
Give extra-special thanks for these extra-special days.
Keep close to your heart
the beauty and the richness of these days.

Smile big and
give thanks for
those amazing experiences,
for those amazing days.

CHAPTER 11

PLACES

Grateful for My Garden

Springtime.

My boys plant wildflowers for me. Soon enough, floral dreams will bloom and will give my heart much joy. I love the way these mixed-seed packages surprise me every year. I don't exactly know what flowers and what colors will greet my eyes in July.

Summertime.

I take a big breath and enjoy the day's presents. Summer suits our backyard well. An invasion of colors, a treat to my eyes. The powerful green of the inviting grass, the symphony of colors in my favorite spot—my wildflower garden. Pink mixes with yellow, white with red. Purple marries orange and magenta.

Can you hear this soul music?

All around, the butterflies chase beauty and collect sweetness. I am getting lost in a sunflower's smile. My fingers become petals.

Thank You, New York City

Before David's era,
exploring the city
felt like a hobby.
Walking on streets with houses bordered by long steps,
popping into a theater to watch an indie movie,
eating a delicious risotto in a tiny crowded restaurant,
enjoying the complexity and
the craziness of this urban dream.

Strolling through NYC feels like
stepping into a movie.
Everyone is in a relaxed rush;
the city's noise mixes with the street smells.
Everything seems alive.
Everything pulses with originality and coolness.

I adore NYC.
Nowadays,
I appreciate more and more
the peacefulness of my Garden State life.

Grateful for Tula Yoga

Being outdoors feels like home to me, but I'm thrilled I also found a place within walls where I can get as high as in the middle of a forest. This place is called Tula Yoga, and for me, it's a heavenly place.

Balance is the magic word when talking about living your best life. *Tula* is a Sanskrit word meaning balance.

I am so grateful for Jen Cavalieri and Jen Guarino for creating such a special space where lots of people can go and enter paradise. I am so very grateful for all instructors at Tula Yoga. They are all amazingly talented, and I just love them.

Some yoga classes are not easy for me. We sweat, we push our limits (our imaginary limits, of course), but the benefits are huge. I enjoy the classes that make me challenge myself, and I adore the relaxed classes when my spirit travels to the core of things.

I am so humbled by these experiences of going deeper into myself, these occasions of connecting my body, my mind, and my spirit. I love to stretch myself. I love to reach to a place in me that has no limits, no time, no fear.

There is an intense bond, a powerful connection between all people attending a certain yoga class. My good vibes mix with the earth's and others' good energies. My peaceful state of mind is beneficial to me and all people. We are one.

Thank you, Tula Yoga! Thank you, beautiful young women (J&J), for creating a portal to the most beautiful world one can imagine.

Namaste!

Grateful for Deep Cut Gardens

Fresh-cut grass tickles my toes.
With every step I thank
Mother Earth for being.

Sky's clear face greets me in the park.
I nod while catching
a sunray under my eyelashes.

Couple of evergreens decorate the lawn.
Their needles, delicate brushstrokes,
smell like forever.

The forest nearby whispers in the wind.
New leaves meet each other
for the very first time.

Birds compose songs on high branches.
I lie down and die for a long moment.
Earth's silence wraps my soul in silk.

The rose garden sends me an irresistible invitation.
Soft pink, red, white, and yellow petals
offer their beauty to the world.

I am breathing green!
Time stops.
My heart blooms.

Grateful for Holmdel Park

Green, everything is green. King Chlorophyll smiles. Being in my favorite park on an early spring day is a great gift I am giving myself.

Sitting on a bench by the lake, taking everything in. Six turtles, maybe a family, sunbathe on the log that's half above the water. When the warm weather settles in, I notice them often resting in this very spot. This time the turtles have an unexpected visitor, a bird. From a distance, I assume it's a black duck, but from up close, I see it's a taller bird with long eyebrows pointing to the sky. I understand the desire to reach up to the blue infinity, but today, the earth's pull is stronger.

I am coloring my soul in this lime green that dresses everything around me. This green tone, specific to the beginning of spring, is such a soothing color, such a dream. I am opening my soul's windows to let all the fresh air invade me.

Birds are drunk with spring fever; they fly from branch to branch, singing their joy. A marmot shows herself briefly before continuing her journey in the tall grass. Mother Nature waltzes. Baby leaves tremble slightly. Long-stemmed flowers tease the bees while moving gently with the breeze.

A woman walks by my bench. She also feels nature's quiet heartbeat. She looks at me and whispers, "Hello." How wonderful strangers greet each other outdoors.

How beautiful it is when we recognize our sameness, our oneness, our shared essence.

King Chlorophyll invites me to dance. I'm flying in his arms. We are floating somewhere between earth and sky, somewhere between "heaven now" and "heaven later."

Thank you, dear Holmdel Park! Every time I visit you, it's Christmas; my soul gets filled with presents.

Grateful for My Favorite Place: My Heart

Living in my head was no good,
so I chose to live in my heart instead.

Living in my heart,
what a wonderful place to be:
warm,
cozy,
always available,
open to all,
eternal,
full of understanding and love.

Love living in my heart!

Dear Reader

Where is your dearest place?
Your home?
A vacation spot?
A beach?
The heart of a forest?
A certain street or boulevard?
Your hometown?

Wherever your favorite place is,
please close your eyes and imagine yourself there!

Give a big fat "Thank you" for your wonderful place.
And don't forget to
visit it often,
for real or in your heart.

CHAPTER 12

REMAIN GRATEFUL

Grateful for All New Things

Grateful for new paths taken,
new roads explored,
new beginnings,
new chances offered,
new dishes at the table,
new flowery dresses,
new books in my hands,
new people in my life,
new rooms to step into,
new thoughts,
new perspectives that will enlarge my horizons,
new poems I'll create,
new gray hairs to teach me acceptance,
new years to come and bring joy, sorrow, and love,
new natural wonders noticed and appreciated,
new skills acquired,
new writing styles,
new places discovered in my heart,
new dust particles,
new songs touching my soul,
new paintings admired,
new wishes made,
new hugs given and received,
new sunsets,

new kisses,

new life lessons,

new healed wounds,

new raindrops,

new ideas,

new leaves in the trees,

new flowers smiling at me,

new days,

new hours,

new minutes,

new seconds,

new you,

new me,

new now.

Being Grateful Is a Choice

Being in love with my life is a choice.
I am choosing to cherish my blessings.
I am choosing to understand and accept my trials.
I am choosing every single day to express my gratitude!

When life pours me a glass of champagne,
When life hands me some lemons,
When life pours me a glass of water,
When life offers me something—anything—
I am choosing to be grateful!

Little by little, "Thank-you" by "Thank-you,"
I've come to realize
I am the one holding the pitcher God gave me.
I can pour myself a fresh drink.
I can choose to keep my glass filled with goodness.
I can choose to be grateful every single day!

Grateful for Today

There isn't a day more beautiful than today.
There isn't a day more precious than today.
There isn't a day more important than today.
There isn't a bigger gift than the gift of this day.

Let's spend this day well.
Let's not waste it.
Let's smile a bit more.
Let's remember we do have wings.
Let's fly.

I am so grateful for being alive today!

"Yesterday is history, tomorrow is mystery, but today is a gift. That is why it is called a present" (Bil Keane).

Embrace the Mystery

What great experiences will I collect today?
What kind of miracles will I witness?
What kind of wonderful can I create today?
How present can I be while traveling
through the next twenty-four hours?

Let's explore this newborn day together.
Let's chase beauty today.
Let's choose kindness.

Let's tell God—
through our words,
our thoughts,
and our deeds—
how much we appreciate,
how joyful we are, and
how grateful we are for
being alive today!

Thank You for Your Beauty

You are beautiful for no reason and
for all the good reasons in the world.

You may be lighter or heavier than
the people who appear on the cover of magazines.

You may have more wrinkles
or more white hairs than a couple of years ago.

You may not be as fashionable, as traveled,
as money rich as the famous stars.

You may not be as schooled, as trained,
as confident, as brave, as ready as others.

Nevertheless, you are
an incredibly beautiful human being!
Yes you are!

You are uniquely made.
You are God on the inside!
You are blessed.
You have heaven in your eyes when you smile.
You have light in you even when you cry and suffer.

Even when the world seems to crumble
to pieces all around you,
the light is still there,
the beauty still in you.

Most of all, what makes you beautiful
are those crazy amazing moments
when you let your light shine bright!

You are the most beautiful version of yourself
when you are unapologetically yourself,
when you live as beautifully as you can,
when you do your best and call it a day.

You are so beautiful when you want to grow
through all life's experiences.

You are beautiful when you are no longer a slave
in the chains of your own mind,
the chains of negativity and fear.
You are a beautiful, beautiful,
beautiful human being.
You are a gift to this world!

Don't try to compare, copy, or compete
with your sisters or brothers.

You are a unique piece of the human puzzle,
and the world is not complete without you!

You are beautiful.
Close your eyes and
know this in your heart!

Thank You, Dear Reader

Wow, you made it to the last page. Thank you for accompanying me on my gratitude journey. I hope my book inspired you to start your own journey of the heart.

Start by saying, "Thank you," for someone or something right now. Can you find ten things you are most grateful for? Challenge yourself. Pretty please. Thank you!

_____

_____

_____

_____

_____

_____

_____

_____

_____

_____

_____

_____

_____

_____

_____

_____

_____

_____

_____

Do not forget that good habits improve the quality of our lives a lot. It does not matter much what we do once in a while. What really matters is what we do on a regular basis.

Thank you, dear fellow human being!

Remain Grateful

About the Author

Alina Adamut dips her pen in soul ink. She met her husband in her twenties, she met her son in her thirties, and she met herself in her forties. *Grateful: In Love with My Messy, Beautiful Life* is her first book, born out of the pains of growing wings and the deep appreciation for all life's blessings. She lives in Hazlet, New Jersey, with her boys and her cat, Daisy.

Printed in the United States
By Bookmasters